THINKING AND ACTING INNOVATIVELY

KEVIN EIKENBERRY

Participant Workbook

Pfeiffer
A Wiley Imprint
www.pfeiffer.com

For additional copies/bulk purchases of this book in the U.S. please contact 800-274-4434.

Pfeiffer books and products are available through most bookstores. To contact Pfeiffer directly call our Customer Care Department within the U.S. at 800-274-4434, outside the U.S. at 317-572-3985, fax 317-572-4002, or visit www.pfeiffer.com.

Pfeiffer also publishes its books in a variety of electronic formats. Some content that appears in print may not be available in electronic books.

Participant Workbook ISBN 978-0-470-50193-1
Facilitator's Guide Set ISBN 978-0-470-50557-1

Acquiring Editor: Holly J. Allen
Assistant Editor: Lindsay Morton
Marketing Manager: Tolu Babalola
Director of Development: Kathleen Dolan Davies

Developmental Editor: Susan Rachmeler
Production Editor: Michael Kay
Manufacturing Supervisor: Becky Morgan

Printed in the United States of America
Printing   10 9 8 7 6 5 4 3 2 1

Contents

THE COMPETENCIES OF REMARKABLE LEADERS

The Remarkable Leadership workshop series is based on the book *Remarkable Leadership: Unleashing Your Leadership Potential One Skill at a Time* and consists of twelve workshops, based on thirteen leadership competencies from the book. (There is no workshop for the first competency, learn continually, as that competency is embedded in all the workshops.) Although you may not be attending the full series of workshops, all thirteen competencies are listed next.

Remarkable Leaders . . .

1. Learn Continually
2. Champion Change
3. Communicate Powerfully
4. Build Relationships
5. Develop Others
6. Focus on Customers
7. Influence with Impact
8. **Think and Act Innovatively**
9. Value Collaboration and Teamwork
10. Solve Problems and Make Decisions
11. Take Responsibility/Accountability
12. Manage Projects and Processes Successfully
13. Set Goals and Support Goal Setting

WORKSHOP OBJECTIVES

After completing this workshop, you will

- Learn to recognize and address common creativity squelchers.
- Understand the connection between your view of mistakes and the creative process.
- Know how to prepare for and conduct a better brainstorming session.
- Understand the creative process and how to emulate creative geniuses.

OPENING QUESTIONS

Ponder, and then write your answers:

1. What do I hope to gain from this session?

2. Am I creative?

Here is a quick assessment to help you think about how creative and innovative you are.

Use the following 1–7 scale on each question:

1 – Almost never   5 – Usually

2 – Rarely/Seldom   6 – Frequently

3 – Occasionally   7 – Almost always

4 – Sometimes

I am flexible.   ___

I am creative.   ___

I support new approaches and ideas.   ___

I put new ideas into action.   ___

I try new things.   ___

Beware of Creativity Squelchers

Cold Water Comments

- That will never work.
- We tried that once.
- It's not in the budget.
- It's too risky!
- That's crazy.
- They'll never buy it.
- Others that you have seen, heard or said:

Why do they squelch creativity?

Other Creativity Squelchers

- Thinking habits/personality types

- Poor team function/dynamics

- Organizational culture

- Too many closed questions

- Time pressure

- Lack of clear purpose or focus

WHAT ABOUT MISTAKES?

- How do you view them?

- How often do you hear about them?

- How does this relate to innovation and creativity?

Environment

- Tactile stimulation
- Add some music
- Toss in some treats
- Get moving
- Go somewhere else

Getting Focused

Seven Ways to Improve Your Brainstorming

■ Warm up.

■ Set a goal.

■ Don't stop.

■ Allow more time.

■ Adapt, modify, and steal.

■ Save evaluation and conversation.

■ Remember the "rules."
- There are no wrong ideas.
- Focus on quantity, not quality.
- Don't stop to explain or evaluate.
- Hitchhike on other ideas.
- There are no bad ideas.

Types of Brainstorming

- Free Wheeling

- Round Robin

- Slip

- Hybrids

- Small Groups

THE FOUR-STEP PROCESS

1. Preparation

2. Incubation

3. Inspiration

4. Evaluation

Are you doing all four?

How well?

- Look at problems in different ways.

- Make novel combinations.

- Force relationships by thinking in metaphors.

- Make thoughts visible.

- Think in opposites.

- Prepare for chance.

- Produce!

Supporting Creativity

1. Try something new yourself. It can be something little, but it needs to be visible. It will be best if you adjust something you are known to have "always done that way."

2. In your next meeting, encourage people to come up with more ideas before deciding on which ones to try. By creating a longer list of possible ideas, better ideas will emerge. Make sure to set the expectation of no "cold water comments" during the brainstorming session.

Better Brainstorming

1. Pick one of the suggestions in this workshop, and apply it in your next meeting.

2. Make notes in your journal of the results, your observations, and lessons learned.

YOUR NEXT STEPS

1. Think back to your goals for being here (page 2). Reflect on what you have learned that you can apply to your situation.

2. Teach a colleague (or your team) this content as a way to solidify your own knowledge and understanding.

3. Be responsible for applying these concepts and ideas in your work and the rest of your life.

4. Ask yourself: "Which Now Steps will I apply *right now*?"

5. Take that action!

6. Commit to your daily application to lock in your learning and achieve greater results!

"We move toward our potential when we turn learning into action."

~Kevin Eikenberry

ADDITIONAL RESOURCES

More innovation tips are provided at **www.RLBonus.com.**

- For a report to help you recognize and reduce the effects of cold water comments, use the keyword "coldwater."

- For a list of personal creativity obstacles, use the keywords "creativity obstacles."

- For specific suggestions on helping a team get past the fear of failure, use the keyword "failure."

- For a list of five ways to warm up your group for greater creativity, use the keyword "creativity warm-ups."

- For a comparison of the various brainstorming methods, use the keywords "brainstorming approaches."

- For a list of random words you can use to trigger creativity, use the keyword "wordlist."